CW00816155

## About the Author

Michael McAllen regrets reaching the age of 80 without making any meaningful contribution to the world – no children conceived or reared, no building designed or built, no sporting or artistic achievements, no vaccines discovered, no export orders gained. These humble verses are the best he has to offer and if anybody should remember more than two lines of any of them, that would be a success.

Michael is a long-term sufferer with Parkinson's Disease.

# MICHAEL McALLEN

# *Princess Ice Cream*

## *and Other Verses from the 1970s*

AUSTIN MACAULEY PUBLISHERS™

LONDON • CAMBRIDGE • NEW YORK • SHARJAH

A CIP catalogue record for this title is available from the British Library.

ISBN 9781398404786 (Paperback)
ISBN 9781398405325 (ePub e-book)

www.austinmacauley.com

First published in this collection 2022
Austin Macauley Publishers Ltd®
1 Canada Square
Canary Wharf
London
E14 5AA

# Acknowledgement:

My brother, Nick, who laboriously typed out the final draft

*Dedicated to Liz Borrett*

# Poems

# Princess Ice Cream

She is a girl of tender years,
Too old for toys, too young for tears.
With eyes of blue and ruby lips,
Lips that could launch a thousand ships!
And in her hair there is no hint
Of rinse, peroxide, dye or tint.
Just long, cascading golden curls
More precious than a sea of pearls.

Her skin is like the finest silk,
Dressed with oils and bathed with milk.
A honeyed voice so soft and warm,
It makes the bees desert the swarm.
While children wait in single file
To taste the sugar in her smile.
And in her veins there runs a stream
Of sweet delicious Devon cream.

Majestic, stately, self-possessed,
A fashion plate divinely dressed.
Miniskirts and summer blouses,
Knee-length boots and winter trousers.
Tiaras, diamonds, royal crowns,
Pyjamas, swimsuits, evening gowns.
Cotton, satin, wool, or lace,
She wears them all with equal grace.

She moves with firm but gentle sway;
No swan could glide in such a way.
Like barley blowing in the breeze,
A tranquil scene of restful ease.
And when she sails along the street,
The traffic stops to view the treat.
Yes, even hardened policemen sigh
And throw their helmets to the sky.

No poet in the land could find
Words to describe a girl so kind;
A heart of gold beneath her breast,
Richer than any treasure chest.
No selfish thoughts or gestures mean
To cloud that countenance serene.
In truth there's nothing can displace
The love that's written on her face.

When she's around, there is no pain;
She makes the sun shine through the rain.
All is music, joy and laughter,
Happiness forever after.
Nightingales and larks rejoice
And sing with operatic voice,
While angels pluck their harps and croon
And stars dance tangos 'round the moon.

History students turn their pages,
Seeking beauties through the ages
Who are worthy to be measured
'Gainst this gorgeous, priceless treasure.
"'Tis all in vain," they soon confess.
"There never was such loveliness.
For few can match and none surpass
This girl with beauty, poise and class."

*1971*

---

*This was the first poem I ever wrote. It was inspired by a very beautiful young girl, who used to parade up and down Prince of Wales Road in Norwich during her lunch hour.*

*Just for a joke I entered it into a National Poetry competition with 300 entries and to my amazement it won 3rd prize, £25, which is about £250 in today's money.*

# One of America's Finest Ambassadors:
# Lee Trevino, Supermex

I learnt the game down in Texas,
And I hits the ball real low,
So I loves to play
On a windy day
When a hurricane starts to blow!

When I started to play the circuit
Them fellas was really dour.
They said my swing
Was the funniest thing
Since Doug Sanders hit the tour

When I took me a shot at the Big One*
I was kinda just prayin' and hopin'.
But I played real well,
And what the Hell!
I won me the US Open!

But I wanna be a real top golfer
So I got me a gentle fade**
But with my magic touch
It don't matter much
If I play with a Club or a spade!

When I tied with Jack for the Big One
They said I hadn't a fat chance.
So I really enjoys
Them newspaper boys
When they danced that Mexican hat dance!

---

\*    1971.
\*\*   A fade is a controlled slice. The ball moves from left to right in the air and stops
very quickly on landing.

Then I took me a trip to Britain*
To win me that lil' ol' pot.
But I burnt my hands
In them Birkdale sands
'Cos my putter got so red hot!

But I just gotta thank Jack Nicklaus:
He helped make me the player I am.
So I said "Thanks, Jack,"
And I paid him back
When I stopped him from doin' the Slam!**

And now I have got an army like Arnie,***
And the people just flock to my door.
Them darlin' folks
Just love my jokes,
And they always come back for more!

Yes, the folks all say I am the greatest,
And they call me Supermex,
'Cause I always smile
And they like my style
When I pocket them winner's cheques!

Now the President writes me letters,
Though I can hardly spell my name.
But there ain't no need
For learnin' to read
'Cause now I am in the Hall of Fame!

If I'd had me an education,
There's no tellin' what I might've done.
Can you picture me
Just as dull as can be
As a Wall Street son-of-a-gun?

---

*    Also 1971.
**    The modern Grand Slam comprises the US Masters, the US Open, the British
Open and the US PGA. In 1972 Jack Nicklaus won the first two, but in the British
Open, Trevino beat him by one shot.
***  Arnold Palmer's devoted fans.

And now I meet the swellest people,
So I never swear nor cuss.
But it's kind of all right
'Cause I'm now so white
That I ride in the front of the bus!

Yes, now I'm a wealthy Spaniard,
As rich as the Kings of old.
And I sit at home,
In my money dome
Just countin' them pots of gold!

*1972*

# One of America's Worst Ambassadors:
# John McEnroe, Superbrat

McEnroe, McEnroe, why do you play
Your tennis in such an unsportsmanlike way?
Your parents must wonder how they ever begat
Such a super-insufferable-snivelling-brat.

You snarl at the umpire and swear at the ref,
Use four-letter words that begin with an "f"
You're arrogant, loudmouthed, repulsive, uncouth,
Such a shining example to American Youth!

Yet the gods gave you gifts that are given to few,
That have raised you on high to a privileged view.
So many admire you, yet no one respects;
Your ego has swollen with inflated cheques.

As king of the monsters you strut round the court,
But the linesmen and ball boys, do you give them a thought?
How much do they earn while they wait and retrieve,
Compared to the millions that you have received?

And if Laver and Newcombe and Rosewall and Roche
Had played with your kind of abusive approach,
Would the game have developed and travelled as far
And would you be now such a superstar?

So McEnroe, McEnroe, why don't you learn
To be worthy of some of that gold that you earn?
For each temper and tantrum just tightens the noose
Of the string 'round the neck of the golden goose.

*1979*

---

*Times change and John McEnroe is now one of the pillars of the sport.*

# Another Dubious American Ambassador:
# Jane Fonda – Just a Squalid Nuisance

*In October 1979, Jane Fonda and her husband, Tom Hayden, were touring America campaigning against nuclear power and big business. One cynic was moved to suggest that Tom and Jane were big business!*

When the Gods on high in judgement sit
On those Hollywood hacks from the Hall of Fame,
I wonder who they'll vote "Best Hypocrite"
Could it be a woman – Jane Fonda by name?

"Big business" is the monster that supplies her needs,
That made her so famous and highly paid.
Yet each time she bites the hand that feeds
It renders immoral her whole crusade.

For if Jesus Christ had behaved like that
With gold from the devil to pave the way,
Would the people have cheered or mocked and spat
And his message have lived until today?

She talks about compassion with a heart of stone
And defends the gangsters of North Vietnam.
And her voice is so harsh with that strident tone,
No glimmer of warmth or care or charm.

If only we could put her in a leaking boat
And set her adrift on the China Sea,
Then perhaps while she struggles to stay afloat
She'll remember her defence of infamy.

But now she's found a new war to fight,
Those barons of the nuclear power brigade.
Were it anyone else, I'd say, "She's certainly right,"
But for her it's all just a vast charade.

For nothing corrupts like the political game,
Especially for a shallow superstar.
Jane Fonda, you're a phoney, and it's such a shame.
Just a squalid nuisance, that's all you are.

---

*Shortly afterwards JF married Ted Turner who is one of the richest men in America. Big business personified.*

# Yellow Socks

I took a trip
On a cruising ship,
And I met a handsome man.
He was really a sight,
All dressed in white,
With a glorious, healthy tan.
We played away
Each sunny day,
And eternal love we swore,
But back in port
This dashing sport
Was really an awful bore,
And worse than that
Was the silly hat
And the yellow socks he wore.
Now an orange or pink
Might cause me to blink
Or shake my head in despair.
But a shaming fellow
In flaming yellow
Was really too much to bear.
I'd gladly be seen
With purple or green,
Though black is the colour I'd choose.
But the sight of a yellow,
No matter how mellow,
Just gives me a touch of the blues.
So remember this tip
If you travel by ship
And a handsome man you should meet.
Don't whimper or sigh
For the light in his eye;
Just watch what he wears on his feet.
And if they are yellow
Then holler and bellow
And ring for the captain or mate
For you never can tell
If all will be well

Or whether you're dicing with fate.
And as for myself,
I'll climb back on the shelf
And wait for my man to appear
If he's mad as a hatter,
It doesn't much matter
As long as he isn't too queer*
And I shan't give two hoots
If he sleeps in his boots
And his clothes are just reeking of beer.
But this much I swear,
If he ever should wear
Any socks of the colour of yellow,
Then come hell or high water,
There'll be more than manslaughter,
For I'll murder that gay* coloured fellow!

*1975*

---

*Inspired by the actress Candice Bergen who had a boyfriend who wore orange socks. According to a press interview she was thinking of dumping him, because it was too much. Nothing rhymes with orange!*

\*    These words are in their true and original meaning.

# But I Love You, Don McLean

It's three o'clock in the morning;
It's a real dark night of the soul.
I feel so sad and lonely,
And the night is, oh, so cold.
So I start to play some records
To try to ease the pain,
But there's only one man who can help me,
And his name is Don McLean.

I don't have a pink carnation;
I don't drive a pickup truck.
I'm still searching for a vocation,
And I'm feeling out of luck.
But when I start to play your music
My dragons are all slain,
So I hope you will forgive me
But I love you Don McLean

The first time that I heard you
I remember how I cried.
For the tears fell all around me
On the day that Vincent died.
Your words were gems of beauty:
You really seemed to care,
And you expressed the feelings
That so many of us share.

I think the heavens sent you;
Such talent can't be true.
And I can't believe "this world was meant
For one as beautiful as you."
But now you'll live forever;
Your songs will never die,
For as long as the world keeps turning
We'll be singing "American Pie"

I wish that I could ride with you
And travel on your star.
You're like a wandering minstrel boy,
Just a poet with a guitar.
But if the skies should ever fall,
There's one thing will remain;
For as long as I have life in me
I'll love you, Don McLean.

It's three o'clock in the morning;
It's a real dark night of the soul.
I feel so sad and lonely,
And the night is, oh, so cold.
But when I start to play your music
My dragons are all slain,
So I hope you will forgive me
But I love you, Don McLean.

*1975*

---

*I went to a Don McLean concert at the Albert Hall and found myself sitting next to a young girl who knew all the words to all the songs and sang along. I hope she finds this and recognises herself.*

# A Girl from Omaha Nebraska

I met a girl from Omaha, Nebraska;
Had a couple of questions I wanted to ask her,
Does the corn grow as high as an elephant's eye?
And the girls, are they all made of apple pie?
And the sun, does it shine from a cloudless sky,
cause the weather there's just perfect, so I am told?
But she said it was not
cause in summer it's so hot
And in winter it's as cold
as Alaska.
Then she talked of Fred Astaire and Marlon, too,
And I said "Pardon me, but Marlon who?
D'you mean that guy who mumbles through his nose?"
But I never miss the chance
To watch that Astaire dance.
I just tingle when I watch his twinkle toes.
So if you ever meet a girl from Omaha, Nebraska,
Here's a couple of questions for you to ask her.
Can you cook with the heat of an August morn?
Can you show me the place where Fred was born?
And the crops do you need a special brand of corn
If you want to tap those riches in the soil?
Then she'll tell you how the grain
Comes spouting from the plain;
It gushes like the oil
In Alaska.

# American Flan

*(With Apologies to Don McLean)*

I met a girl who sang off-key,
And I asked her if she'd marry me,
But she just cried and made a scene.
And I went down to the old drugstore
Where I'd often bought some pills before,
And I bought a giant box of Benzedrine.
And in the streets the people jeered,
The p'licemen snarled, and the poets sneered;
My heart was really broken,
I couldn't keep from chokin'
And the three things that I liked the best
Are my cowboy boots and my buckskin vest,
And I have to confess I was half undressed
The day the music died

So bye-bye, Miss American Flan,
Drove my Buick to the music of a rock and roll band.
And them good ole boys were drinking beer from the can,
Singing, "This is just the life for a man;
This is just the life for a man."

Did you write the Book of Vice;
Could you deny the power of Christ
If the devil tells you so?
And do you believe in flaming hell?
Can music cast an evil spell
If you listen to it on the radio?
And I know that you're in love with him
'Cause I saw you take a midnight swim;
You both kicked off your pants,
Man, you really seemed to dance.
I was a lonely, teenage craven creep
With a blue gardenia and a beat-up Jeep,
But I have to admit I was fast asleep
The day the music died.

So bye-bye, Miss American Flan, etc., etc.

Now for sixteen years no grass has grown,
The seed was weak and just badly sown,
So now we use a stronger plant.
And the joker played for the king and queen
With the poker face of Steve McQueen
And a voice that came from Cary Grant.
And while the queen was with her maids
The joker trumped the king of spades;
The courtroom was dismayed,
He'd badly overplayed.
And while Jagger read a book on Jude,
The Stones were playing in the nude,
And we sang hymns of gratitude
The day the music died.

 We were singing,
 "Bye-bye, Miss American Flan," etc., etc.

In the flowering hour of a summer shower
The birds flew off with Eiffel Tower,
Six miles high and flying free.
At last it fell on the fourteenth tee;
The players tried for a birdie three
While the joker in the Clubhouse laughed with glee.
Now when the sergeant used his rifle butt
As he tried to make a vital putt,
We all got up to jive
Cause he made a bogey five!
And as the players tried to leave the course
The cavalry arrived in force
And carried them off in a flying horse
The day the music died.

 They were singing
 "Bye-bye, Miss American Flan," etc., etc.

And there we were all lost in gloom,
A generation steeped in doom
With no one left to lend us cheer.
So Jack, be clever and Jack be clear;
Jack jumped over the chandelier
Cause light is the devil's only fear.
And as I watched him on the screen
My eyes were filled with tears unseen;
No poet locked in verse
Could stop that fatal curse.
And as the cloud rose high into the sky,
As all around prepared to die,
I saw Satan singing "American Pie"
The day the music died.

    He was singing (well almost),
    "Bye-bye, Miss American Flan," etc., etc.

*1975*

---

*I never got round to writing a new beginning, so I took the new ending and stuck it on the front. I'm quite proud of the sublime nonsense of the first four verses! "American Flan" doesn't really sound right, but it's better than "American Beefburger"!*

# Nobody Danced with Me

*'As a certified wallflower, she eschewed junior proms as a potential chamber of horrors; she could will herself into a psychosomatic illness whenever New Year's Eve reared threateningly at the end of the calendar... A re-release of* Gone with the Wind *offered her a four hour lease on heaven... 'It was me up there and all those attractive men pursuing me.'"*

From *Streisand,* by Rene Jordan

If you've ever been a wallflower
Then you'll know just how it feels,
How you smile to keep your courage
And the fear that it conceals.
I was just that kind of girl then,
I had no beauty they could see,
And I cried a million tears when
Nobody danced with me.

I used to go to all the movies,
And I would see myself up there,
How the men would all pursue me
And they danced like Fred Astaire.
But I was not that kind of girl then,
I was as plain as plain could be,
And I died a million deaths when
Nobody danced with me.

Well, I got to make some movies,
Had lots of men pursuing me,
And I danced with Robert Redford;
Just how lucky can you be!!
But I still remember times when
A Brooklyn belle I'd never be,
And I can still hear the chimes when
Nobody danced with me.

*1978*

# Words of Wisdom

As Samuel Johnson once said – or at least,
If I'm wrong, you'll please pardon –
"But a cow in the field is a wonderful beast
But we turn her out of a garden."

*1979*

# Long Live Hollywood

Hollywood, you bore us all to tears,
No decent movie in 20 years.
Vulgarity, violence, lack of mind,
And sex encounters of the grossest kind.
A place where only money talks,
Yet there used to be men like Howard Hawks
And Capra and Hitchcock and Wilder, too,
And many others with a talent true.
But now there's nobody there can write
An original script for our delight.
No warmth or affection, romance or style,
Just nothing to make our spirits smile.
It's enough to break an actress's heart
As they search, without hope, for a female part.
Yet before Women's Lib got underway
There were always feminine parts to play!!
But producers tread their idiot ways
While men of taste avert their gaze.
And jackass actors take their cheques
And sate themselves with drugs and sex.
Such empty vessels, yet so much noise,
No whispered words from the Bedroom Boys!
It's a place where hope eternal springs,
Where cabbages masquerade as kings,
And the only question that we fail to see
Is how they ever got into this industry?
Well, just meet the right people and soon you'll be
A producer for a major company!!
Who cares if you're totally ill-equipped
To write your name or read a script!
No taste, no talent, no style, no wit,
But with moron movies, it doesn't matter a whit.
But no self-respecting writer could work
For a semi-literate kind of jerk.
'Twould be the very height of humiliation
To seek his approval for a work of creation.
Would a writer show his script to a local baker
Or grocer or butcher or candlestick-maker?

But in Hollywood that's what you're expected to do!
(You don't believe it? I assure you it's true.)
So the first thing a writer must understand:
There's mad hatters a-plenty in this wonderland!
They meet at Ma Maison; it's tea they're drinking,
And they're trying to do some original thinking!
"Hey man," said the Hatter while the March Hare grinned
Let's make a new version of *Gone with the Wind*.
With Alice as Scarlett and Dormouse as Rhett,
We can make it the kinkiest version yet.
There'll be sex in the teapot at a quarter to four
And sex in the bathroom and sex on the floor.
And sex on the table and sex in the pool,
While sex in the icebox is beautifully cool!
Atlanta is burning but nobody cares;
We'll have sex on the sofa and sex on the stairs.
Then the dormouse emerged with voice dripping wet:
"Get Streisand for Scarlett and Beatty as Rhett.
Just think of the millions, those beautiful cheques,
With Streisand for beauty and Beatty for sex!"
But a Jewish O'Hara! Most certainly not!
So the dormouse was stuffed right back in the pot.
Then they all changed places and counted to ten,
For the hatter was clearly thinking again –
"We'll do a rock version of *Casablanca*,
With the Stones and Jagger and ex-wife Bianca.
There'll be sex in the desert and sex at the bar
And sex in the back of a Vichy car."
Then a strange voice was heard, like an anguished moan:
"For Christ's sake, just leave these old movies alone.
'Remakes' and 'remakes' is all that I hear;
Doesn't anyone ever have a new idea?"
But producers are people with penniless minds,
Their wealth so excessive it dazzles and blinds.
But thank God they have money – it's all that they've got!
Will they make it to heaven? Most definitely not.
And thank God for the writers wherever they be,
The sick and the starving and the lonely (like me)*
No beach house or ranch house, no mansion or two,

---

\*     Only half true! But alas, I couldn't think of a better rhyme for be!

27

Just a room with a bed and a dismal view.
No pictures, possessions, or Cadillac cars,
Just crumbs from the tables of the movie stars.
But thank God for the actors, with brains that lie fallow,
Stupid and selfish and stingy and shallow.
And thank God for the ladies, nothing tinsel or tawdry,
Like Barbra and Shirley and Julie and Audrey.
Their talent lies wasted; 'tis a pitiful plight;
Their kind of story there's no one can write.
So like rich Cinderellas they wait for the call
Of the prince who will carry them off to the ball.
But, as everyone knows, they've been waiting for years;
The orchestra plays, but no pumpkin appears.
But now the clock strikes twelve and the night draws on,
And almost all of the talented people have gone.
And nothing is left – so what more can be said?
"Long live Hollywood," but Hollywood's dead!

*1979*

# Hollywood Charm

*According to an interview given to Newsweek magazine, Meryl Streep first met Dustin Hoffman when she was an unknown actress auditioning for a play he was directing. He introduced himself with a belch and proceeded to put his hand on her breast. Understandably, she thought he was an obnoxious pig.*

When Meryl Streep met Dustin Hoffman,
His hand on her breast she didn't dig.
"I wish to God you'd take it off, man;
You're really just an obnoxious pig."

*1979*

# They're All Getting Richer while the Movies Get Worse

*It's now clear, too, that the film-student generation – Bogdanovich, Friedkin, Spielberg, De Palma, Scorsese and others – had learned everything about film, and nothing about life. The result has been a cinema that is formally extraordinarily sophisticated at the same time that it is intellectually pre-adolescent.*
James Monaco in *American Film Now*


They used to make movies that had warmth and style,
But we ain't seen too many of them for a while.
For now it's all movies full of space-age toys,
Just adolescent movies for adolescent boys.
But there's no use complainin' 'bout this Hollywood curse,
'Cause they're all getting richer while the movies get worse.

When you think of all the remakes and the movies that they've ruined,
Well, there ought to be a law just to stop them from doin' it.
Another law to save us from American corn
And the twenty-fifth remake of *A Star is Born*.
But there's no use complainin' 'bout this Hollywood curse,
Cause they're all getting richer while the movies get worse.

It's a ripoff business, and there ain't no hope
While they try to make movies the way you make soap.
There's lots of fancy colours, and the packaging's fine,
But its adolescent soap made for adolescent minds.
But there's no use complainin' 'bout this Hollywood curse,
'Cause they're all getting richer while the movies get worse.

All the stories seem repulsive and the characters so phoney,
Sorta glorified bunkum mixed with Hollywood baloney.
The mind gets corrupted, easy livin' on the Coast;
Got no time for conversation, they just talk about the gross.
So there's no use complainin' 'bout this Hollywood curse,
'Cause they're all getting richer while the movies get worse.

No, here's no use complainin'; take it east and relax,
With their two-bit talents and their tired old hacks.
The money boys are rulin' in this town without a heart;
It's the movie business, baby, and it sure ain't art.
So there's no use complainin' 'bout this Hollywood curse,
'Cause they're all getting richer while the movies get worse.

Well, I guess you get the picture, for it sure is plain
That the train to the coast is the Gravy Train.
If you ain't got talent, it don't matter a dime;
It's a paradise for parasites all o' the time.
So don't start complainin' 'bout this Hollywood curse,
Just grab your share from this well-stocked purse,
Where they're all getting richer while the movies get worse.
Yes, all getting richer while the movies get worse
And worse and worse and worse.

*1979*

# Tribute to Veronica Lake

*(Miss Peekaboo)*

Miss Peekaboo,
I loved you true;
Perhaps you might have loved me, too,
If only I'd been there to care for you.

I curse my fate.
I found you thirty years too late.
Time wouldn't stop, you couldn't wait,
And now I say a silent prayer for you.

O Hollywood, you had no heart.
You let this lovely girl depart,
Who graced your shallow movie art
With so much charm.

A precious jewel on display,
She sparkled in a special way,
But this priceless gem you threw away
Without a qualm.

Miss Peekaboo, etc., etc.

Too many hearts were broken there,
Too many men who didn't care,
Too many girls who found despair
When fame had passed.

The music stopped on the merry-go-round,
And in a sea of drink she drowned,
So now I thank the Lord she's found
Some peace at last.

Miss Peekaboo,
I loved you true
Perhaps you might have loved me, too,
If only I had been there to care for you.

I curse my fate,
I found you thirty years too late,
Time wouldn't stop; you couldn't wait,
But how I wish I had a lock of hair from you.

1975

---

*She was the only actress I ever fell for. I had no idea she was so tiny. In fact so many actresses are very tiny. I think there must be a biological reason.*

# In Memoriam

*(Written after reading* Montgomery Clift, *by Patricia Bosworth)*

His life was brief,
But he found his role,
And death brought relief
For his tortured soul.
He touched our hearts
With his special gift,
A Master of Arts,
Montgomery Clift.

*1979*

# Impressions from the Movies

*(But False, I Hope!)*

In the USA you will not find
The smallest child of any kind.
For the children there, precocious dears,
Are just miniature adults of tender years.
But amongst the adults you will find
Millions of children of every kind.
Confused and vulnerable, full of fears,
They're sometimes children for fifty years!

*1979*

# Help Me Make It Through the Day

*(For Woody, one of America's oldest children!
Inspired by the movie* Manhattan.*)*

My analyst has gone away,
I'll never make it through the day.
I'm like a sheep that's lost its way,
A hunted, wounded stag at bay.
My wife has left me – says she's gay!
Please help me make it through the day.
A million dollars? I'll gladly pay
If you'll help me make it through the day.
On bended knees I'll even pray
To try and make it through the day.
But I'd rather have a bed and an easy lay,
For I feel much better when I hit the hay.
And the girls in Manhattan just love to play,
To help me make it through the day.
But at forty-two I'm turning grey
While she's seventeen if she's a day!
There must be, surely, an easier way
To help me make it through the day.
I wonder what the people in England say
As I strive to make it through the day.
"Nutty as hell!" Is that what they say?
O God, what a dark, depressing day!
But perhaps I should try it the English way,
With cups of tea from a silver tray
And cricket bats that kept Hitler at bay
Whilst I struggled through my Brooklyn day.
But bombs and rockets, come what may,
I'll somehow make it through the day.
I'm a natural coward, I'll avoid the affray
And live to fight another day.
But at last there's hope – or at least a ray –
For my analyst comes back today.
He's quite insane, but he comes from LA
Where it's kind of normal to be that way.
And when I hear his voice, I shall be okay,

And together we'll struggle through the day.
For there's nothing so good as to hear him say,
"Please help me make it through the day!"

*1979*

# Thoughts on Orson Welles

*A good director is someone who doesn't annoy you*
Howard Hawks

*Helicopter shots, I don't mind – but not in the living room, please.*
Billy Wilder

The greatest movie? Well it's perfectly plain.
What else could it be but *Citizen Kane*?
For critics and phonies all tell us the same,
And movie historians give sim'lar acclaim.
So its fame keeps expanding. How enormous it swells,
'Til it's almost the size of Orson Welles!
But forgive me for saying , if I may be so bold,
That I find it so heavy and horribly cold.
It's all too depressing, a cheerless refrain,
No warmth, and no women to soften the pain.
But I mean no discredit, and I try not to scoff,
But whenever I see it I soon turn it off.
For you cannot expect any great works of art
From "genius boy-wonders" quite lacking in heart.
And I can never see just what is so great
'Bout the camera angles, that plain irritate.
Was ever a director so much overrated,
Top heavy with genius or just overweighted?
And his talent for writing was really quite small;
In fact he was really no writer at all.
But, in truth I don't aim to belittle his size;
I just think it's his voice where his genius lies.

*1979*

# God Almighty, Never Again

*(Dedicated to all those who silently suffer in the cause of "Art")*

*Theatre has become esoteric, you only go there now if you are a bit odd.*
                                        Robert Urquhart (Actor)


I once had to sit through an Ibsen play;
Spare me, O Lord, from that dismal pen.
It took four hours, and it seemed like a day;
No, never, never, never again.

If I remember right, it was called *Peer Gynt*,
Full of mad Scandinavian men.
I nearly died from that four-hour stint;
God Almighty, never again,
No, never, never, never again.

I once had to sit through a Strindberg play,
Another lot of sad Scandinavian men.
I went right down on my knees to pray,
God Almighty, never again,
No, never, never, never again.

I once had to sit through a Chekhov play,
Full of miserable, moping men.
"Please take up tennis," I wanted to say;
God Almighty, never again,
No, never, never, never again.

I once read a play by Bernard Shaw;
Preserve us, Lord, from that promiscuous pen.
Has there ever been a greater bore?
God Almighty, never again,
No, never, never, never again.

(In fairness, perhaps I ought to say
*Pygmalion*'s a really wonderful play,
But that's an opinion you may not share
If you didn't much care for *My Lady Fair*.)

I once had to sit through a Williams* play
Full of sad homosexual men.
How I wished those guys could be a little bit gay!
God Almighty, never again,
No, never, never, never again.

I once had to sit through a Pinter play,
Full of mad, unspeakable men.
I just couldn't repeat what I wanted to say;
God Almighty, never again,
No, never, never, never again.

I once had to sit through a Marcus play,**
The story of a middle-aged lesbian hen.
I'd rather hear a turkey sing any day;
God Almighty, never again,
No, never, never, never again.

If you ever had to sit through an Albee play;
Just hold your breath and count to ten.
You might even hear the Mad Hatter say:
"God Almighty, never again,
No, never, never, never again."

I once read a play; it was called *The Front Page*;
Enjoyed it so much that I read it again.
No power on earth can keep me from that stage;
God Almighty, just tell me when,
I'll go again and again,
And again and again and again.

*1975*

*     Tennessee.
**    *The Killing of Sister George* by Frank Marcus.

# Free Verse

I've just been down to the local libr'y,
Read a book of modern verse.
Random thoughts from every season,
Poems with no rhyme or reason;
Can't help wonderin' who they're pleasin';
Seems to be so easy.
But I must go back to the local libr'y,
Find a book by Robert Frost.
Words of his that should be set down:
"Verse that's free is such a letdown;
Tennis playing with the net down
Would be just as easy!"

*1979*

# To A Lady on Her Forty-First Birthday

*(Imitation of Dr Johnson's famous poem to Mrs Thrale: "At Thirty-Five". As befits a lexicographer, the rhymes were, of course, in alphabetical order.)*

Forty's gone, and life's begun
Now that we are forty-one.
Never think that life is done
When you're only forty-one.
Take your partners, have some fun;
Sex is better at forty-one!
Grab your rifle, get your gun,
Be fighting fit at forty-one.
No more cloisters like a nun,
'Tis bad to be alone at forty-one,
For there's so much more of life to run,
When you're only forty-one.
But watch your diet; it's time to shun
Those fattening foods at forty-one.
And avoid the heat of the midday sun
To retain your youth at forty-one.
And don't be jealous – no girl of twenty-one
Can ever match a woman of forty-one.
So relax and be happy; the battle's won;
You've finally made it to forty-one!

1978

---

*Mrs Thrale was the wife of a rich brewer, who was a benefactor to Dr Johnson in his later years.*

# To A Movie Actress on Her Forty-Second Birthday

*(Another Johnsonian imitation.)*

As Shakespeare once said, it's "much ado
About nothing" at all to be forty-two.
No need to be worried and never be blue;
It's time for adventure when you're forty-two.
You can sail the Atlantic in a small canoe
If you feel so inclined at forty-two.
You can ride on the back of a kangaroo,
For it's never too late at forty-two.
But don't lie on the beach out at Malibu
And waste "the summer of forty-two".
And never wear a blouse you can see right through;
It's time to be demure when you're forty-two,
Be simple, be natural, and to yourself be true;
Be a beautiful woman of forty-two.
And remain please, forever just the lady "who
Stole my heart away" at forty-two.

*1978*

# Song for Cole (Porter)

*Every nation derives its highest reputation from the splendour and dignity of its writers.*

Samuel Johnson

When I was seventeen years old
I heard a song that touched my soul;
It was Ella singing the words of Cole
And really hand in glove.

And something very strange occurred
As I listened to each magic word,
For I knew at once that I had heard
A message from above.

And ever since that fateful day
When "Uncle" Cole showed me the way,
I've always wanted a chance to say
A word of thanks – and love.

So let's begin at the very beguine
In a gay, romantic 'twenties scene
At a time when anything goes.

And imagine a beauty named Samantha,
But, alas nobody could romance her,
"For my heart belongs to Daddy."

But then one day she met a male
Who had oceans of love for sale,
And he told her, "You're the top.

"And your body I crave,
So let's misbehave
All through the night".

And though she had to agree,
"You do something to me.
It's the wrong time and the wrong place".

But every night and day
He called to say,
"Mind if I make love to you"?

"And you know that it's true
I get a kick out of you,
So let's do it; let's fall in love".

"And in the still of the night
Just let me hold you tight
While I concentrate on you."

Then she was heard to sigh;
"So in love with you am I
That I've got you under my skin.
"And I thank my lucky star,
For it's more than wunderbar.
It's delightful; it's delicious; It's d'lovely."

But soon a change in her condition
Required a visit to the physician,
Who promised a little one.

And from that night of joy
She gave birth to a boy
But it was just one of those things.

Then her lover spoke with passion,
"I'm always true to you in my fashion,
But please don't fence me in.
"And although I want to cry
Ev'ry time we say goodbye
I've just got to get out of town."

And from this moment on
Samantha sang this song;
"What is this Thing called Love,
This Funny Thing Called Love?"

But soon she found a new love,
And he spoke to her of true love:
"You'd be so nice to come home to."

"And I swear by the gods above
You'd be so easy to love,
'Cause your sensational; that's all."
And although they were very poor,
It was love for evermore,
And, after all, who wants to be a millionaire?

But they prospered as the years went by,
And soon Samantha was ridin' high
In that beautiful high so-ci-e(u)-ty

*1975*

---

*Includes references to some 35 of Cole Porter's most famous songs.*

# Always Knew You Had It in You, Baby

*(A Songwriter's Lament)*

Nobody wants to help you when you're struggling;
Nobody wants to give you the time of day.
They just wait until you've made yourself real famous,
And then they'll come around – Here's what they say:
"Well we always knew you had it in you, baby,
And your talent – why, it stood out a mile."
And they flatter you with lots of fancy contracts,
And they flash you with that phoney business smile.

So many record firms turned down the Beatles,
And Don McLean, turned down by thirty-four!
I could tell you what they said about Bob Dylan,
But I kinda think you've heard that song before.
But talent is so rare they never meet it,
So you can't expect their judgement to be right,
And most of them are blind as bats and barn owls,
So they cannot recognise it in the light.

If you read the lives of all the greatest writers
I guess you'll find it's always been that way.
They just wait until you've made yourself real famous
And then they'll come around – here's what they say:
"Well, we always knew you had it in you, baby,
And your talent – why, it's like we always said."
I'm just thankful that I never took up painting
Cause they'd never recognise me till I'm dead!

*1975*

# The Day I Joined the Band

I went down into the cellar to check the fire escapes,
And I came across Bob Dylan makin' the Basement Tapes.
I said, "Bob, how ya doin'?" but he didn't understand,
Cause he was plugged into that music he was playin' with the Band.
Yes I really dug that sound
Hewas makin' underground,
And I asked him if I could play.

Then he threw me a guitar and said, "Join us if you can."
I said, "Bob, if you don't mind, I'll be your tambourine man."
Then I was caught up in the web that he started to spin,
And I felt just like a feather that was blowin' in the wind.
Yes, I really dug that sound
We were makin' underground
In that basement hideaway.

Then a beautiful, barefoot girl appeared; she wore flowers on her
    head.
And ol' Bob glanced up at her. "Just like a woman," he said.
And we began to tease her, "Sister, where's yo' shoes?"
But then she started to sing "The Subterranean Blues".
Yes she really dug that sound
We were makin' underground
And she begged us to let her stay.

Well, she had real cool hands that sort o' caressed the piana,
And Bob led us slowly into "Visions of Johanna".
Then he revved his guitar and said, "Let's have some fun,"
So we raced along Highway Sixty-One.
Yes, I really dug that sound
We were makin' underground;
It was a special holiday.

Well she got pretty worked up as she started to play,
But Bob calmed her down: "Lay, lady, lay."
And she recovered her cool: "Don't think twice, it's all right.
But I'm feelin' so high I'll be your baby tonight."
Yes, she really dug that sound
We were makin' underground;
It just carried her away.

And so the music rolled on, like a rolling stone,
And we picked at our guitars like a dog picks a bone.
No, I shan't forget that day when Bob showed us how,
And I feel like Baby Blue 'cause it's all over now.
Yes, I really dug that sound
We were makin' underground;
Man, we really made some hay.

But things are seldom what they seem,
And I have to confess it was all a dream.
And nobody seems to understand
When I talk about the day I joined the Band.

*1975*

# I Don't Have A Thing to Wear

## *(A Woman's Lament)*

I've got wardrobes full of dresses,
Closets with no room to spare;
Yet my life an awful mess is;
I don't have a thing to wear.

All these other lovely women,
They seem dressed without a care.
Wish I hadn't started slimmin';
I don't have a thing to wear.

I've got millions of shoes
That I never use;
I've got bangles and bits;
But nothing fits.
I've got sixteen houses
Full of skirts and blouses,
And scarves by the mile,
But they're out of style.
And I just don't know what I'm gonna do;
I feel as if my life is through.
Just a lady with no means,
Reduced to jeans.

And when my lover asks me out to dine,
I think of how I'll fix my hair.
"But, darling," I answer, "I must decline.
I don't have a thing to wear."
I went to London, and I met the Queen,
And this is what she said, I swear:

"I've got more clothes than you've ever seen,
But I don't have a thing to wear.
No, I don't have a thing to wear."

*1978*

# Love Is the Feeling that I Have for You

Love is gentle, love is wise;
Love is the light in a woman's eyes.
Love is the sound when the angels sing;
Love is the gold of a wedding ring.
Love is a smile that ever charms;
Love is a babe in a mother's arms.
Love is giving, never getting;
Love is remembering, not forgetting.
Love is honour, love is bold;
Love is never bought and sold.
Love is divine, celestial blessing;
Love is sharing and not possessing.
Love is the grace of a Grecian goddess;
Love is always pure and modest.
Love is the truth and can never lie;
Love is alive and will never die.
Yes, love is forever and love is true,
And love is the feeling that I have for you.

*1972*

# A Woman's Lament

"Adultery," said Jesus, "is always a sin."
And I sure understand what you said, Lord.
But sometimes I feel that I'd love to begin
The beguine with that gorgeous man Redford.

*1979*

# Girls with Sunglasses

*(With Apologies to Dorothy Parker)*

Men seldom make passes
At girls with sunglasses.
For when she hides behind a screen,
A girl can see but can't be seen.
And though she acts with much aplomb,
She's really just a Peeping Tom!

*1975*

# Another Famous American Liberal

## (Lillian Hellman)

*George Will, writing in* Newsweek *magazine, suggested that if Lillian Hellman had defended Hitler's tyranny for fifteen days in the way she defended Stalin's tyranny for fifteen years, she would have been branded forever as a scoundrel.*

Lillian Hellman, Jewish Liberal,
Chronicled her scoundrel times.*
Yet Lillian Hellman, Jewish Devil,
Defended ALL of Stalin's crimes!

*1979*

* *Scoundrel Time* is the title of Hellman's autobiography.

# Just a Grand Passion

I don't want no placid love affair.
I want to touch the stars: I want to walk on air.
I want to feel the current running through my hair:
I want a grand, grand passion.

I want the kind of love to set my soul aflame.
I want to dance with nature so I feel no shame.
I want a wild affair; I want nothing tame.
I want a grand, grand passion.

I want to love like the greatest lovers of old.
I want no silver affair; it's just gotta be gold.
I want no timid caress; I want those kisses bold.
I want a grand, grand passion.

I want to be like the heroes in the books we read;
I want to ride with love on a coal-black steed.
I want a goddess of love; that's all I need.
I want a grand, grand passion

I want to hear those harps while she sings me psalms;
I want to bathe in the beauty of her body's charms;
I want to lie in the warmth of her loving arms;
I want a grand, grand passion.

So give me a palette, and let me try
To paint a picture of love in a rainbow sky.
I want a splash of colours before I die.
I want a grand, grand passion,
Just a grand, grand passion.

    Wow!

*1975*

# Two Single Beds

When boy meets girl, their one desire
Is a place to lay their heads.
But they wouldn't dream of lying in
Two single beds.

"If this is love, we must have more,"
And so the couple weds.
But they wouldn't dream of buying
Two single beds.

Alone at last, they tread the ground
That every couple treads.
But they wouldn't think of trying it
In two single beds.

But as the years roll gently by,
The passion slowly starts to die.
And routine sex gets to be a bore;
It's just another marital chore.

And she complains, and how she moans
About his awful grunts and groans.
His want of charm, his cold caress,
His brutal lack of tenderness.

While he regrets her fading beauty,
Her sad neglect of wifely duty.
And though he loved her once so dear,
He'd much prefer his glass of beer.

And though 'tis sad, they both admit,
The romance is (all) in shreds.
And now they're simply dying for
Two single beds.
And now they're really sighing for
Two single beds.
Yes, now they're almost crying for
TWO SINGLE BEDS!

*1975*

# Clinical Sex

*According to Masters and Johnson, most heterosexuals are bumblers in their lovemaking. The doctors suggest that sexual partners be treated with consideration, understanding, and unhurried gentleness.*

Ten thousand members of the population
Have performed the act of copulation
In front of the cameras and under the lights;
In the name of science, ten thousand delights!
Heaving and breathing, they lunge and lurch
To aid the cause of sex research,
While Masters and Johnson with solemn pose
Record the sexual highs and lows.
No time to admire a well-shaped bust
As they measure the power of the pelvic thrust.
No time to applaud each new orgasm
As they measure the heartbeat, pulse and spasm.
Just anchors aweigh and organs erect,
All the facts and figures double-checked.
But what have they learnt after all this time,
That sex is ridiculous or truly sublime?
For surely by now they must have discovered
Many a graceful and elegant lover?
But, sad to relate, their report reveals
They were clumsy as a pack of performing seals!
For it seems that these thousands of sexual tumblers,
In the art of love, were sexual bumblers!
And so what is the secret of sex success?
"To proceed with unhurried gentleness!"
And so all this research has finally shown
What every woman has always known!

*1979*

# Have You Ever Seen a Feminine Feminist?

Have you ever seen a feminine feminist?
No, of course you ain't – she don't exist.
Search around the world, and all you will find
Is a hard-faced lady with murder on her mind.

Never seems to smile, no sense of proportion,
Never talks of anything except abortion.
Never seems aware that her one-track mind
Just renders her one of Hitler's kind.

So preserve us, Lord, from these awful creatures,
Their mixed-up minds and masculine features.
Banish them to Belsen or some similar place,
And send us, please, some women with a human face.

*1979*

---

*Nowadays every woman seems to think she is a feminist, but she bears no resemblance to the original.*

# Let's Kill the Mothers Instead

## *(Abortion Blues)*

I guess I was a nuisance, too much trouble to give birth,
So I never saw the starlight nor the beauties of this earth.
And now I'm just a foetus, and I'm permanently dead,
And I never got a chance to die a peaceful death in bed.
So forgive me if I say something that really should be said:
Let's kill the mothers instead.

I might have been a Shakespeare or a Shelley or a Keats.
They might have built a shrine to me and statues in the streets.
But now they'll never know about those poems in my head,
For they killed me for convenience and I'll be a long time dead,
So forgive if I say something that really should be said:
Let's kill the mothers instead.

They talk of mothers' feelings, and they talk of mothers' rights,
And abortion's there to free them from the errors of the night.
So they murdered me in comfort, and they prospered while I bled,
For I was just the error from the pleasures of the bed.
So forgive me if I say something that really should be said:
Let's kill the mothers instead.

Yes, they killed me very quickly; it was really very neat.
And they had no time to marvel at my little hands and feet.
They just put me in a furnace till I turned a glowing red,
And they really didn't care about the blood and tears I shed.
So forgive me if I say something that really should be said:
Let's kill the mothers instead.

*1975*

---

*I'm not a raging anti-abortionist, but we may have lost an awful lot of geniuses.*

# Square Tomatoes

*Scientists at the University of California have developed a square tomato! It has a tough, flat-sided skin, which makes it ideal for picking by machine. It is also extremely resistant to bruising while being packed for shipment. It has now become the standard tomato for canning.*

God in his wisdom so profound
Decide to make tomatoes round,
But the scientists this view don't share,
And much prefer to make them square!
For it seems the canning boys have found
Machines don't like tomatoes round.
And farmers, too, have found it pays
To interfere with nature's ways.
And so with crass, commercial haste
They alter shape and ruin taste,
And no one apparently seems to care
If they make tomatoes round or square.
But I can't help wondering where it is leading,
This ghastly business of genetic breeding.
What horrors are they planning while we slumber:
A square banana or square cucumber?
And how sad that science should so demean
Those gifts of nature, just to fit a machine.
But if vegetables can be humbled so to fit the can,
It's easy to imagine what's in store for man!

*1978*

# If You Want to Win

*(Inspired by Gary Player)*

A golfer, he needs
Lots of seaweeds.
Pacific kelp's
A terrific help.
Nova Scotia dulse
To balance the pulse.
It's the iodine
Gives the hair a sheen,
And I think you'll find
It clears the mind
And makes a man much wiser.

And may I repeat,
"You are what you eat."
So it's wholewheat bread
To be well fed,
And rich proteins
Like soya beans,
And salads lined
With every kind
Of vegetable known,
Just as long as it's grown
With compost fertiliser.

And never use pills
To cure your ills,
No Aspirin
If you want to win.
The body it wrecks
With its side effects,
For only mugs
Resort to drugs.
It's gotta be wrong,
For they don't belong
In the world of our creator.

But honey serves
To soothe the nerves,
So never lean
On nicotine;
While alcohol's
No good at all.
But if one ignores
Nutritional laws,
It's a certain bet
That man will get
Sickness sooner or later.

*1972*

---

*Since I wrote these words Aspirin has proved successful in preventing heart attacks.*

# Juggernaut Blues*

If you travel down our country lanes
You'll often chance to find
A herd of thundering juggernauts,
With a traffic jam behind.

They hog the roads, both sides at once,
And charge like buffaloes,
And anything that bars their trail
Just gets a bloody nose.

They ride like conquering armies through,
In clouds of diesel smoke,
And no amount of fumes can make
Our politicians choke.

These feeble-minded, flanneled fools
Just flex their flabby muscles.
"I'm afraid it isn't up to us;
These laws are made in Brussels."

And these Common Market** bureaucrats –
Well, they don't understand.
They think our roads were built for tanks,
The way that Hitler planned.

But one man knew just what to do
When other methods fail,
And with a book he learned to shake
A Molotov cocktail.

And soon he finds a lonely giant:
Like a naval queen she sits.
And with his bomb he really blew
That bloody thing to bits.

*    In Britain, large diesel trucks are commonly referred to as "juggernauts".
**   The Common Market (The European Economic Community) is a preposterously bureaucratic organisation, which Britain joined in 1973 in the mistaken belief that it would guarantee unlimited prosperity!!!

It really was a juggernaut bang;
'Twas heard for miles around.
And everywhere the people cheered
The leader they had found.

And when the police arrested him,
His tears he could not hide.
But none of them will ever know
His tears were tears of pride.

And now he sits within his cell,
With lots of time to lose.
And there he wrote this soulful song
And called it "Juggernaut Blues".

*1975*

# London, City of My Youth

London, city of my youth,
You've lost your charm: you're so uncouth.
Forgive me if I speak the truth:
It's just my acid pen.
You're a jungle of cement and glass:
Your architecture's all so crass.
O God, I never want to pass
This way again.

But, yes, I know what's wrong.
I've been away for far too long.
And now I really don't belong
Here anymore.

But my, how things have changed,
And all the streets seem rearranged,
And all the faces look so strange
To me.
There's polished tin for burnished gold,
And the things I loved now leave me cold
And all the young girls look so old,
But can it really be?

But yes I know what's wrong.
I've been away for far too long,
And now I really don't belong
Here anymore.

I walk the streets and feel so sad,
And the frenzied traffic drives me mad:
Yes, I admit, I'll be real glad
To leave this awful place.
For it seems that everyone consumes
A deadly diet of diesel fumes;
How I miss the country's sweet perfumes,
And its easy gentle pace.
And its quiet, human face.

But yes I know what's wrong.
I've been away for far too long,
And now I really don't belong
Here anymore.

*1975*

---

*A deadly diet of diesel fumes – No improvement in 40 years.*

# The Mediterranean Sea

*(Written after watching a television program.)*

If you want to see what man can quickly spoil,
Then walk the shores of Europe, washed with oil,
Where the sewage lies around for all to see
As it helps to kill the Mediterranean Sea.

And the Lord above looks down and wonders why
We let the ocean's gentle creatures die,
And why the fish are full of mercury,
And why we have to kill the Mediterranean Sea.

But the scientists pursue their lethal ways
In their search for new and wondrous toxic sprays.
But a good supply of oil and DDT
Is enough to kill the Mediterranean Sea

And the businessmen haven't the sense to realize,
As they push their precious plans to industrialize,
That the waste they make is killing you and me,
Just as it kills the Mediterranean Sea.

When chol'ra calls or we catch the typhoid fever,
Then the UN boys all fly off the Geneva.
But the politicians there just can't agree,
So they let us kill the Mediterranean Sea.

I wish that I could wave a magic wand
To try to save this stinking sewage pond.
But alas we can't escape reality
As we rush to kill the Mediterranean Sea.

And when the sea is dead and nothing grows,
Then tourists stay at home and hotels close.
For who wants to go to Sunny Italy
When we've gone and killed the Mediterranean Sea?

*1975*

# Down South America Way

## ( Inflation Blues )

*There were two general elections in Britain in 1974. As a result of the first, Labour returned to power with a very narrow majority. Accordingly, another election was held in October. At this time, inflation was approaching 20 per cent and still rising. It was painfully obvious that neither Harold Wilson nor Ted Heath had the remotest understanding of its cause – or cure. In a moment of despair, I wrote the following:*

O God above, won't you send us please
A man with the wisdom of Socrates?
We're tired of these piddling mediocrities
Who don't know what they're doin'.
They speechify all day
In their birdbrain politician's way,
But they never hear what the people say
As they lead us all to ruin.

So wake up, Harold, and wake up, Ted,
And remember what Abraham Lincoln said.
How long do you think we can afford
Politicians who practise criminal fraud
On the people of this land?
I've got to tell you that we're mighty sick
Of this goddam government confidence trick
That's getting out of hand.

We pay high taxes, but we're still not through
'Cause we've got to pay for inflation, too.
And if there's anything left, it's hard to use,
For just try to save and you're bound to lose
The rest of what you earn.

But these barrel-headed government guys
Don't realize why prices rise;
They think they can cure them with subsidies,
But that's an awful joke.
And some of them just can't understand
Why things never work out as they planned,
But they're all of them living in cuckoo-land,
These Simple Simon folk.

And though I'm just an ordin'ry guy,
I'll gladly tell you the reason why.
It's all a question of the money supply,
As Enoch always knew.
When governments get themselves into a mess,
They always resort to the printing press,
But they never, never, never confess
For the damage that they do.


When inflation bites, then they try to ease
It with a wages pause and a prices freeze,
But if you start a flood then you cannot stop
It with a tin-can bucket and a kitchen mop.
But still they never learn.

And now the flames reach higher and higher,
But still they pour paraffin on the fire.
When it comes to money, they never tire
Of spreading it around.
There's a typhoon blowing, it's a nightmare trip,
And every sensible rat is abandoning ship,
But old steel ball Queeg takes his strawb'ry sip
As he runs us all aground.

When supplies run out and there's kids to be fed
And a million pounds won't buy a loaf of bread,
Then I guess we'd all be better off dead;
We'd better start to pray.
So get out your guitars and join this song,
For the road will be hard and very long;
We may not make it, but I hope I'm wrong
Down South America way. Olé!

---

*Unable to find a suitable male, God sent us a woman instead!*

# A Nation in Despair

*When Harold Wilson retired as Prime Minister and leader of the Labour Party in 1976, the London* Daily Telegraph *wished him "all happiness in his retirement" and noted that he was mainly responsible for leaving behind "a nation near bankrupt, living on tick, sinking under a preponderant bureaucracy, almost defenceless, all effort, skill and achievement savagely penalised, all shiftlessness rewarded, its best citizens reduced to despair or emigration."*

Once we had an empire,
Governed half the world,
And every time the sun rose
The British flag unfurled!
A spirit of adventure,
A nation strong of heart,
However could that spirit
So quickly fall apart?

First we lost our empire,
Then we lost our way;
Now we're just decrepit,
A study in decay.
Lost our sense of freedom,
Lost our strength and will,
Drugged by tranquillizers,
A nation on the pill.

Governments print money;
Prices hit the roof;
Bureaucrats proliferate
With pensions fireproof.
Crushed by legislation,
Taxed beyond belief,
No one to ease our burdens,
No one to bring relief.

Drowned by regulations
In a sea of tight controls,
Which like a mighty ocean
Forever onward rolls.
Trapped in all our dealings
By that cursed VAT,*
Soon we'll need permission
Just to make a cup of tea!

Think of all the heroes
From our glorious history,
Then gaze upon the row of boobs
Who run the TUC.**
Dreary, aged, petty men,
Enough to bring on tears,
Haven't had a new idea
In all of forty years.
Parliament is riddled
With the meanest party hacks;
Our leaders fall behind them
And follow in the tracks.
The communists are laughing
At our nation in despair;
A Solzhenitsyn warns us,
But does anybody care?

1976

---

*I was not regretting the loss of Empire, but merely wondering how we ever had the energy and enterprise to run it! At the height of its power, Britain ran the whole empire with 128,000 civil servants. By the late 1970s, it took over 700,000 just to run Britain alone!!*

\*     Value Added Tax (A small-businessman's nightmare).
\*\*   TUC – Trades Union Congress.

# I Wish I Were in England

### *(Thoughts of Emigration: Things That I Would Miss)*

I wish I were in England now that June is here.
I'd be gambling down at Ascot in my fancy racing gear.
Though I laugh at all the fashions and the way-outlandish dress,
It's a precious part of England, and it's racing at its best.

> Let me dream, let me dream
> Of those rich, red strawb'ries and cream.
> And those lovely summer evenings when the daylight lingers on.
> Oh, I wish I could recapture the summers that are gone.

I wish I were at Wimbledon to tread the hallowed grass.
I'd be drinking in the atmosphere like champagne from a glass.
Though I'm passing thirty, forty, still I hear the umpire's call,
And I miss that lonesome whistle of a Connors cannonball.

> Let me dream, let me dream
> Of those rich, red strawb'ries and cream.
> And those lovely summer evenings when the daylight lingers on.
> Oh, I wish I could recapture the summers that are gone.

I wish I were at Canterb'ry to watch the cricket there.
I'd be sleeping through the ritual in that cool cathedral air.
But I'd waken for that charmer, that dark and dashing thief;
Just to watch him steal a single, it's the magic of Asif.*

> Let me dream, let me dream
> Of those rich, red strawb'ries and cream.
> And those lovely summer evenings when the daylight lingers on.
> Oh, I wish I could recapture the summers that are gone.

I wish I were in London just to walk down Regent Street.
I'd be feeling like a prince of wealth, the riches at my feet.
But of all the world's possessions, well, I'll gladly trade my share
Just to hear that nightingale that sang in Berkeley Square.

---

\*    Asif Iqbal – a fleet-footed Pakistani who played for the county of Kent.

Let me dream, let me dream
Of those rich, red strawb'ries and cream.
And those lovely summer evenings when the daylight lingers on.
Oh, I wish I could recapture the summers that are gone.

*1976*

---

*Confession time: I've never been to Ascot or Canterbury or Berkeley Square. And it's twenty years since I was last at Wimbledon!*

# I Wish I Were American

## (With apologies to Ronald Reagan)

*"So dependent is he on speechwriters, in fact, that he even assigned a group of them the task of writing the famous eulogy he delivered for Bobby at St. Patrick's Cathedral."*
From *Ted Kennedy: Profile of a Survivor*, by William H. Honan

I wish I were American, and then I could be
A candidate for the US Presidency.
I'm sure I'd be the only one to write his own speeches,
And I guess that's mighty rare – as history teaches.

A man who would be President of the USA
Shouldn't need a dozen writers to tell him what to say.
But if you really want an actor, as many others have been,
Then you might as well get Redford, or Reynolds, or McQueen.*

A poet in the White House? It might be better by far
Than a shop-soiled senator superstar.
For it takes a man of vision to lead the nation by the hand,
And a man without a dream will never find that promised land.

Good looks are not sufficient, nor a fashionable name;
The stakes are far too high, and it's no family football game.
For character's essential, and it's very rarely found
In a man who would abandon a woman who has drowned.

But the poor will not abandon him, but do they really care
For the pseudo-understanding of a multimillionaire?
Much better try to understand the economic laws
And when speaking of inflation to understand the cause.

But the greatness of America is the people and the land,
And I pray you'll never turn those golden prairies into sand.
So if I could run for President, I'd forget about the oil,
But I'd fight to preserve the currency and fight to protect the soil.

---

\*     This was of course, written before the death of Steve McQueen.

But it's just a foolish dream, of course. It certainly cannot be:
You must be born American to seek the Presidency.
But, America, please forgive me if my question seems unkind;
But a middle-aged delinquent – is this the best that you can find?

*1979*

# Anna and the News at Ten

*(With apologies to Reginald Bosanquet)*

"Howdy, folks, well, here we go again
And this is Anna Ford with the *News at Ten*.
There's death and destruction all around
And the usual trouble with the doggone pound.
Slaughter on the highways – well you know what it's like,
And the ambulance boys? Yep, they're all on strike.
While there's rain in Bangladesh – two million drowned –
And a million umbrellas in the Lost and Found.
But, man, it's real sad and I almost cried,
For it's the biggest disaster since Elvis died.
But if you want good news – well, it's tough luck, pal,
'Cause I ain't no honey-voiced good-time gal.
Just a sharp-shootin' sister with no time for fun
'Cause my daddy always told me, "Annie, get your gun."
But tune in tomorrow for some good news, maybe;
There'll be a real surprise from old "Reggie baby".
He'll be all dolled up like a Southern dude,
With a toupee on his head and the rest of him nude.
With a couple of broads to clear the bourbon fog,
For old "Reggie baby's" a real hot dog.
But now we'll take a break and after then
I'll be off to see Magnolia at Number Ten.
I swung m'hips at Mark* but he was kinda bored
'Cause my low-slung chassis's not his kind of Ford.
I guess he knows the feel of a racing moll,
But he oughta take the wheel of a real live doll!
And now we're off to Thailand – at least Alastair** and I am,
Where "Anna, shall we dance?" said the handsome king of Siam.
"Well, it's mighty fine, King, but excuse me please,
'Cause we're here to meet them starvin' refugees.
They've been livin' on grass – so the folks all say,
And though it's better then grits, it sure ain't hay."
And now for the late news – it's a football score:

---

\*    Mark Thatcher, son of Margaret, was a part-time racing driver.
\*\*   Alastair Burnett was a fellow newscaster.

Liverpool nil and Arsenal four!!!*
Well, I'll be a cotton-pickin' son-of-a-gun;
Fancy Liverpool losing – four goals to none!
But that's all for now, folks, till tomorrow at one,
And don't miss Reggie; he'll be lotsa fun!

*1979*

---

*The nineteen-seventies was a decade of disasters, wars, bombings, assassinations and strikes. There were in fact, at least three full-scale wars, twelve invasions, ten major terror organisations, and coups or attempted coups in over 110 out of 201 countries known to the currency exchanges. At least forty presidents, prime ministers and heads of state were deposed.*

*In Britain, despite inflation, ever-rising unemployment and abysmal political leadership, we did, however, manage to avoid a military coup, although we had more than our fair share of strikes. Indeed, the decade ended with the "winter of discontent", when millions of local government and hospital workers, including the ambulance men, went on a prolonged strike against the Labour government's wage-control policies. To a certain extent, like the rest of the nation, they were sorely provoked, but the callousness displayed by these supposedly "caring" people left many of us deeply shocked.*

*Inevitably, the nightly television news in Britain, and presumably elsewhere, became an endless catalogue of disasters. The fact that it was now increasingly presented to us in soft feminine tones did not make it any the more palatable. However, with their endless changes of earrings, brooches, hairstyles, neck scarves, and so forth, this new breed of newscasters did manage to distract us from some of the worst horrors. And having proved that women, too, were sufficiently talented to be able to read an autocue, they quickly became major national stars. Among those who rode to fame and fortune on this female bandwagon was Anna Ford – very solemn, very beautiful, and very English – who quickly followed her fellow newscaster, Reginald Bosanquet, as a permanent fixture in the gossip columns. But whereas Reggie, toupee firmly fixed, was famous for his frequent difficulties with wine and women, for Anna the problem was simply, and endlessly, men!*

---

\*    Liverpool was the champion English soccer team through much of the 'seventies; they practically never lose a home game. (The author, of course, is an Arsenal supporter.)

# Beware

They told us that Thalidomide was perfectly safe,
But that didn't last for long.
They said that DDT was perfectly safe,
But of course they got it wrong.
They tell us that sodium fluoride in the water is perfectly safe,
Though it's banned in other nations.
And now they tell us that nuclear power is perfectly safe,
Though it may destroy creation.
But how can they banish all our fears
When the wastes are lethal for thousands of years?
And how do they really expect us to feel
When they store it in tanks of stainless steel?
For the future of all of our lives are at stake;
All it takes is a bomb or perhaps an earthquake.
And there never can be a scientific solution
To the horrors of radioactive pollution.
So let sanity reign; let wisdom prevail.
Let's round up the scientists and stick them in jail.
This world is too precious, and they do not belong
Until they have learnt what is right and what's wrong.
And remember, in matters of nuclear fission
Politicians are people with limited vision.
They care nought for tomorrow; they live for today.
So you cannot believe anything that they say.
And most are so old that they really don't care
If they poison the water and poison the air,
For one thing is certain: they won't be there!
So beware – and beware – and beware.

*1975*

# In Good Sir Peter's Golden Days

*In an interview given to the* Sunday Times *in 1980, Sir Peter Hall (director of the National Theatre) suggested that the last twenty-five years had been a glorious period in the field of British Arts – "a neo-Elizabethan age"!!*

In good Sir Peter's golden days
When Shakespeare bowed to Pinter's plays
And Mozart wept on bended knees
To marvel at our symphonies,
And every poet on the streets
Could match the words of Johnny Keats,
And buildings rose into the skies
All Jerry-built with subsidies,
No Gothic spires or Norman towers
Just glass and steel and plastic flowers
To decorate the concrete domes
And make the patrons feel at home,
And opera's billowing thunderclouds
Gave hearty voice but much too loud,
And phoney actors strode the stage,
Where sodomy was all the rage,
And every artist knew the tricks
Of arranging piles of wood and bricks.
O good Sir Peter, prince of men,
'Twas heaven to be alive just then!

*1980*

# The Girl with The Billowing Hair

*(Bus Stop Blues)*

"She rides in beauty like the night",
A trail of billowing hair.
And I often wonder where she goes
And I wish that I was there.
And though she often looks at me,
Dishevelled, down-at-heel,
I wonder if she really knows
Exactly how I feel.

But I'm too old, too ill, too poor,
And creaking at the seams!
Too many years that went astray,
Too many broken dreams.
But when old mem'ries fade away
There's one 'twill never part.
I'll still recall that girl who rode
Her bike into my heart!

I wonder what became of her;
I never knew her name.
Perhaps she rode into the wind,
Extinguished like a flame.
I hope she found a man to care,
To love her tenderly.
And though I shouldn't say these words;
I wish that man was me.

*1978*